WITHDRAWN

COLORSCAPES

COLORSCAPES

INSPIRING PALETTES FOR THE HOME

Susan Sargent with Jill Connors

Photography by Eric Roth

BULFINCH PRESS
New York · Boston

Bulfinch Press

Hachette Book Group USA
1271 Avenue of the Americas
New York, NY 10020
Visit our Web site at
www.bulfinchpress.com

First Edition: November 2006

Library of Congress Cataloging-in-
Publication Data
Sargent, Susan.
    Colorscapes: inspiring palettes
for the home / Susan Sargent,
with Jill Connors; photography by
Eric Roth.—1st ed.
        p. cm.
    Includes index.
    ISBN-10: 0-8212-2868-4
    (hardcover)
    ISBN-13: 978-0-8212-2868-5
    (hardcover)
    1. Color in interior decoration. 2.
Interior decoration—Psychological
aspects. I. Connors, Jill. II. Roth,
Eric. III. Title.

    NK2115.5.C6S263 2006
    747'.94—dc22

        2005035847

Design by Dania Davey

PRINTED IN CHINA

To all the colorful people and houses along the way

CONTENTS

INTRODUCTION

Why do most people live with the colors of mud, dust, fog, and soot? I have no good answer to this question. The range of colors available today—in paint, wallpaper, fabrics, and home accessories—is astonishing, providing a veritable garden of delights to feed the souls of chromophiles. There is enough variety—from the subtlest pale shades to the most exuberantly loud—to suit every imaginable taste. Color has been declared the design element du jour by magazines and television decorating shows, and the Internet has made it possible to find any product at all, no matter how exotic—yet beige and white still dominate most interiors.

I think we have been brainwashed by real-estate agents ("You can't sell a house if it isn't white"), decorators ("sophisticated" = safe), and retail stores and catalogs that sell the easiest colors to coordinate (the predictable neutrals). Despite our growing understanding of the inspiring, welcoming effects of color, we still have trouble stepping beyond the threshold of bland to put it all together. As a lifelong color fanatic, I myself admittedly pull colors together by instinct, without relying on rules or formulas. I find most decorating theories both ponderous and dogmatic; I prefer pictures to words. As a designer, I add colorful elements to my collections and my home to suit my own taste. When asked to analyze what I do, I worry that too much navel-gazing may inhibit my natural bias toward free-ranging experimentation.

Still, I regularly give talks and conduct workshops on using color, and I promote a liberating color message along with my home-furnishing collections. I strongly believe, first, that color is intensely personal, and second, that all rules are made to be broken. Yet I also recognize that it is all too easy to become overwhelmed, and that even avid color enthusiasts may stop short of implementing their ideas for lack of confidence. To assist you in that regard, I want to share a number of useful, nontechnical procedures and "almost-formulas" I've developed that can help ensure success. Identifying techniques for getting organized can relieve some of the anxiety of a choose-it-yourself project and empower you to make colorful choices.

My mission is to present a variety of interiors—some professionally planned, some not—each of which shows a distinctive point of view. The color palettes illustrated range from luminous to quiet, reflecting a wide range of personal tastes. These ideas can be adapted to many different situations, and I hope you will find them inventive and inspiring rather than elaborate or intimidating. This multitude of variables should not be discouraging—just the opposite! The point is that on each project, the homeowner or designer took risks, suffered setbacks, made adjustments, and finally succeeded brilliantly. This book is intended to serve as an encyclopedia of exploration, encouragement, and even exhilaration as you expand your own color thinking. All the advice included will support your efforts while allowing for a large degree of flexibility and personal creativity.

While I am a vocal color advocate, that does not mean that I think "Just go for it" is always the right guidance. Using more colors—and particularly bold ones—poses its own challenges. For instance, color can have such a strong presence that too many distractions—fancy trim, layers of swags, cluttered tables—can cause visual chaos. Walking into an overly colorful room can be like walking into a chattering crowd at a party. If the noise level is too high, you can't focus on the conversation. The brain can absorb and visually understand a limited number of shapes and colors, so the level of color you use needs to reflect and respect that reality. The Japanese word for restraint, *shibuis*, refers to knowing when to stop. Planning is the key to getting any project started and on the right track.

MOOD BOARDS

How do we get comfortable with starting, adventuring, and experimenting? Color selection becomes much less overwhelming when you approach it in an organized way. In my experience, the most essential step in planning is to assemble a "mood board." Mood boards come in many shapes and sizes, from the obsessively rigid (an array of same-size swatches neatly pinned in straight rows) to the resolutely chaotic (a swirl of paint chips, snips of fabric, feathers, postcards, and photos of dream rooms).

Think of it this way: a mood board is your room in miniature. It can be a binder, a shoebox, or an actual bulletin board, but whatever form it takes, it's where you'll record all the ideas you have and stash the materials and color references that appeal to you. (I also sometimes find it helpful to take digital pictures of the room I'm working on, from each direction, to use as a guide.)

As you organize and edit your thoughts, the mood board will become your evolving plan. Nothing is written in stone—remember, it's your tool, not your boss. Be ruthless in your editing if you find yourself with too many options, but be brave if you feel yourself slipping back toward beige. This is the place for you to play out your fantasies.

A mood board can also help you determine how much color you really want to live with. You may well discover that you want to stop short of full immersion. With a mood board, you can explore your color convictions. So, if we reduce the process to percentages:

A *10 percent starter step* might amount to adding some color to a neutral room with a couple of bright pillows and a throw.

A *40 percent change* could mean committing to painting a color on the walls.

A *60 percent face-lift* would allow for a colorful rug along with the new paint and pillows.

A *100 percent makeover* would be the works: painted walls, rug, and upholstery.

(*Note:* If you are 0 percent committed, do *not* read this book!)

I've provided photographs of mood boards for many of the rooms featured here. They show the palettes that were used and, in some cases, the color inspirations that began the process. Observing how a mood board connects to its room will get you thinking about how color ideas are planned and integrated.

COLOR SELECTION

Gender, culture, and personal experience all inform the way each of us perceives colors; there are as many perspectives as there are people. The challenge—and the thrill—is to create a unique color plan by identifying our preferences and relating them to our homes.

Within each chapter, a section titled "Color Ingenuity" examines the color concepts that came into play. In some cases, a precept was deliberately followed to create the room; in others, the design may have been less consciously executed but nonetheless, illustrates a sound approach.

COLOR INGENUITY

Here is a brief summary of some of the ideas you will encounter in the book.

1. **CONTRAST: A room without contrast is flat and unappealing.** Think of a black-and-white photograph: the black and white at the ends of the spectrum are what animate the grays in the middle. It's the same process in a room: the contrast of dark and light colors heightens the color effect. For instance, black is a vibrant background for hot red; it makes the red pop. Contrast both brightens and lightens colors, as well as emphasizes shapes—as with a dark sofa set against a light wall. Contrast can be created using the dark and light versions of a particular color or using complementary opposites. It can refer to a dissimilarity in color or in material (wood against wool, chrome against chintz).

2. **TEXTURE: Sometimes texture can have as much impact as color.** Texture can be either tactile (woven fabrics, wood, plaster, stone) or visual (reflective surfaces, such as glass or metal). It's important to have a mix of textures in your fabrics. Avoid using only flat, printed materials or many similar weaves. Texture and the mix of materials become especially essential in colorful interiors, where they will create interest and depth. Without them, a room runs the risk of being cartoonishly flat or one-dimensional.

3. **COLORS WITH NEUTRALS: Adding some quiet tones can both support the underlying color scheme and give relief to the eye.** Don't get so focused on color that you forget to leave some blank space in the room. (This is easy to do—I have to check

myself all the time.) The inclusion of some neutrals can correct any excesses in a too-colorful room or, conversely, can provide a background for a more restrained color story limited to decorative accents. An excess of neutrals, however, will always be dull.

4. **SPLASH: Use color in one strong dose for maximum effect.** Try out a mural or a single decorated wall instead of painting the whole room. Minimizing the color zone can allow you to be bolder in your color choices without compromising any other elements you already have in place.

5. **COLOR FAMILIES: Using multiple shades of a single color can be effective.** Several shades of yellow paint, for example, can travel in sequence across a series of rooms. If you're planning a room around a

single color, make sure that all the materials in it—fabric, paint, and floor covering—are using the same take on that color. In other words, green is too broad. You need to refine your focus, as in bright green, olive green, lime green, and build up your color family within that specific grouping. Take it one level deeper. Kelly green is not a good match with lime green or olive. But a range of olives from soft to deep will work very nicely.

6. **TRANSITIONS: Think globally.** The passage from room to room within your home must be coherent and logical from a color standpoint, not abrupt or jarring. Carrying one color along, even as a minor accent, will link the rooms together. The color of a bright cushion can be repeated on a doorway or in a throw rug in the next room.

7. **COLOR PARTNERS: A warm color paired with a cool color is a simple way to start.** Most of us don't want to decorate our homes in simplistic primary colors, so we pick more complex shades that shift off the standard color wheel. When pairing a cool color with a warm one—blue with red, for instance—try to look for a blue that has some tint of red in it, and a red that has a tint of blue. This will tweak both colors and bring them closer together. Alternatively, you can go for a red and a blue that have both been softened with a touch of gray to tone them down. The gray will integrate them. Avoid pairing a sharp color with a muddy one, because both will suffer. As a general rule of thumb, your two colors should have equal presence and equal influence.

8. COLOR BALANCE: Are the colors on your mood board soft and restrained or bold and vivid? Building a mood board with actual swatches will help you decide how to balance the colors you've chosen so that one won't overpower the others. Colors change depending on the company they keep, so always consider how one affects another. Give yourself some time: let the mood board sit for a bit while you keep trying different combinations and variations, until you're happy with what you see.

9. THINKING IN THREES: Picking a three-color palette. "Thinking in Threes" is a good way to narrow down your choices and begin to focus. First, put together three colors you like. Next, identify which elements in the room are going to be "recolored" and consider how much of each color you want to use. The primary color should be on about 60 percent of the elements, the secondary on about 30 percent, and the accent color on about 10 percent. Suppose your palette is teal/blue/lime. Your rug contains several shades of teal, so you pick up on that color and paint the walls with it. You can also find decorative pillows with a teal print. Blue is your secondary color, so that becomes your choice for the upholstery fabric on your sofa, with a different blue fabric for the two armchairs. Since lime is your accent color, you might use it on a couple of lampshades, as well as on the trim on the pillows. These percentages are flexible, and you may want to add extra colors as the work progresses.

You will learn more about these color ideas, and many others, in the pages that follow. I hope you will be inspired by the work of the color-loving interior designers and homeowners whose rooms are shown here. The common feature of all these interiors is the clear sense they convey of adventurous fun. Take this approach away with you and keep an open mind. Giving yourself some time to think your ideas through—letting yourself experiment, relax, and enjoy the process—will work better than following all the rules in the world.

Susan Sargent

1.
color
inspiration

THE PROJECT: A practical farm couple restores and invigorates a country home.

THE COLOR SCHEME: Citrus yellow, spring green, lavender blue, teal, apricot, and red

THE INSPIRATION: Colors from the surrounding landscape, flowers, and mountains

WHAT WENT RIGHT: This light and airy house with many windows could take a lot of color.

BEST FEATURE: The green and blue mudroom has a built-in floor sink for cleaning boots and bathing the family Golden Retriever.

JUST FOR FUN: Golden yellow walls impart an upbeat feeling to a newly added living room on the west side of the house.

n the years since Sabrina and Tom Warner moved to New England from Tennessee and bought an old farm at the top of a hill, they have restored the original building, room by room, and reconfigured much of the house to accommodate both their teenage children and their large library. It was an ambitious undertaking, but Tom, an architect, and Sabrina, an avid gardener and a very handy woman, were not deterred by the extended commitment involved.

GOLD RUSH: The living room, an addition to the west side of the house, gets its bright outlook from warm, golden walls and white woodwork. A roomy sectional sofa, upholstered in natural linen, faces the fireplace and the built-in television cabinet. The embroidered and appliquéd cotton pillows can be mixed and matched on all the living-room furniture.

The work list has grown steadily shorter, although the floor of the master bedroom still needs sanding and there are a few windows waiting for new sashes. But with the end in sight, Sabrina began to address her decorating plans. Tom had turned an attached garage into a combination mudroom and sunroom, and Sabrina—fresh from attending a color workshop—chose a cool combination of spring green and lavender blue.

VIBRANT ACCENTS: The colors of the appliqué pillows *(left)* echo the red and yellow scheme.

SPACE SAVER: In many houses, the space under the stairs becomes a closet and the dumping ground for mismatched skates, shoes, and sports gear. By building bookcases *(above),* the Warners created both a graphic architectural statement and additional space for their large library. The red walls of the dining room can be seen through a doorway.

What happened next was not unexpected. "You do one room, and then all of a sudden you can't wait to do the rest of the house," says Warner. So when a living room addition on the west side of the house was completed, right around the time of her birthday, Sabrina treated herself to a color gift: she hired painters for the sunny room and picked a vivid hue straight out of an orange grove. "It was a little scary at

SPLASH OF COLOR: Bead board paneling in spring green, and lavender upper walls bring color to the hardworking mudroom *(above)*, where Sabrina Warner gives her cooperative Golden Retriever, Brookie, a bath in the built-in floor sink. The practical slate-tile floor is perfect for a family that keeps backyard livestock and whose members are liable to troop in and out carrying bridles and buckets.

HALLWAY HUES: The back hallway *(right)*, with its antique bench, has green slate floors and a bank of coat closets to the left of the window.

first," says Warner of the moment when the color began to cover so many square feet of wall space. Now, however, the room is the favorite gathering spot for the whole family. Versatile sectional sofas and decorative accent pillows provide an ideal spot for talking, reading, or lounging, and built-in bookcases make clever use of the space under the staircase at one end of the room.

As the color makeover continued, the basic palette of spring green, lavender, and citrus yellow was augmented with sky blue, teal, apricot, violet, and plum in other rooms and on the screened porch. "I love color; it's been so much fun to bring it into my house," says Sabrina Warner. "Once you start, you go way beyond white walls."

THINK GREEN: The green grass and young leaves of early summer were the color inspiration for the sunroom *(left),* where several shades borrowed directly from nature are used for the walls, the wicker chair cushions, and the rug. In keeping with the theme, the sofa fabric is a floral pattern, and the dotted rug suggests seeds or other whirling natural forms.

ON THE PORCH: Bead board ceilings painted blue are a tradition in Vermont, and the Warners preserved theirs when they enclosed the porch on the north end of the house *(overleaf).* The glass panels are replaced with screens in summer; children's art decorates the walls.

COLOR INGENUITY: COLOR INSPIRATION

FINDING THE STARTING POINT FOR YOUR COLOR PALETTE CAN BE THE MOST DIFFICULT STEP

Selecting a palette can seem overwhelming, but if you need a starting point, Mother Nature will seldom lead you astray. Look at practically any pretty home textile pattern, and you'll find that nature has inspired the design.

In this country house, the Warners and their designer live in close harmony with gardens and plants. Designer Jennifer Johnston-Gawlik runs her own perennial business in the summer months, and Sabrina has an extensive garden that she plans and cares for herself. Naturally, the colors and subtlety of garden plants were their inspiration.

The breadth of nature's colors offers something for every taste. Color inspiration does not always arrive spontaneously,

but you can approach it like any other project, with thought and reflection. Your point of reference might be nature, but it might just as easily be colors from another culture (for example, Greek pottery or the painted buildings of Rajasthan) or the latest fashion trends from Paris. A color palette can be borrowed from another period—art deco or Georgian England, for example. The goal is to find a starting point that will allow you to create a palette tailored to a specific location and your personality. Once found, your inspiration should allow you enough variety to build from and provide enough coherence to guide you forward.

2.
contrast

For interior designer Marian Glasgow, all color and design decisions begin with a concept. "I asked the homeowners to conceptualize what they wanted for their home," she explains. "They told me, 'the key word is *zany.*' With that boisterous word in mind, Glasgow chose a palette of blue, orange, and yellow for the first floor of the house, an old city dwelling that had been opened up and given a simplified floor plan in an earlier renovation. Facing the street, the living and dining rooms flank the center staircase. A large eat-in kitchen with a

A LIVELY HELLO: In the living room, just off the entry, royal blue walls and a bold blue and white fabric make a strong visual statement. An area rug in blocks of dark plum, reinforced by matching pillows, gives the palette an extra twist.

breakfast table, a pantry and bar area, and an attached family room make up the entire back of the dwelling.

Throughout the house, cramped interior dividing walls were removed, though the original footprint remains intact. Structural columns were boxed in and decorated with classic moldings to redefine the rooms and provide visual interest. Adding the new color scheme to the rooms created just the right energy.

The living room shimmers with a one-color palette of vibrant and intense royal blue. "The reason to go so vivid in

STOP AND LOUNGE: A mustard yellow chaise *(above)* offers a comfortable place to rest in the sitting area of the second-floor hallway. The sheer white drapery has a leaf motif embroidered in metallic thread. The plaid cushion integrates the chaise and wall colors.
RUNNER-UP: A colorful flower-bouquet motif on the carpet *(opposite)* adds a burst of pattern to the main stairway, whose wainscot, risers, and balustrades are all painted white.

MOOD BOARD: Inspirations for the dining room's palette were contemplated by assembling a mood board *(opposite)* with such elements as beads, berries, fabric, and a painted ceremonial mask.

PLAYING UP THE HUE: A glaze on the painted walls of the dining room *(above and right)* gives the citrus orange the extra depth and richness needed to counter the gleaming white woodwork. Says interior designer Marian Glasgow, "The trim in the room is so strong, we used the color glaze to balance the white." The synthetic silk drapery fabric and the wool area rug introduce a khaki green hue, while the polished wood table and dark wood chairs add another neutral tone to the mix.

KEEP IT LIGHT: The family room, an extension of the kitchen, has a bright and happy feeling thanks to its sunny yellow wall color. Plaid drapery fabric, a multicolored rug, and cheery furniture—including two tomato red leather ottomans—emphasize the room's informality. The decor combines the three major colors in the house's overall palette: blue, orange, and yellow.

the living room is to emphasize the intimate nature of the room, and to have immediate visual impact," says Glasgow. The primary fabrics used on the chairs and sofa pick up the same shade of blue in a print on a white background. Across the hall, the dining room was given rich orange walls, painted with a glaze for extra depth of color. In the sunny yellow family room, the plaid window treatments—in appropriate shades of blue, orange, and yellow—incorporate the entire color scheme. "When the whole house works together like that," notes Glasgow, "you can relax and really live in your space."

PLUM SPOT: A loveseat covered in grape velvet provides a spot for lounging and reading *(left)*. The fabric covering the 40-inch-round ottoman plays up the palette of heathery purple and linen, with a striped button furnishing an appealing accent.

SERENE RETREAT: Because it includes an area that was formerly a sunporch, the master bedroom boasts a wall of windows. Stationary drapery panels define the gaps along the wall between the windows, while sheer linen Roman shades ensure privacy. The fabric chosen for the drapery and the headboard, a contemporary take on paisley *(above),* inspired the room's color scheme of heathery purple, sage, and linen white.

COZY LODGINGS: The guest bedroom's more traditional look *(above)* has been achieved through the use of such familiar and classic patterns as toile and subdued checks. Repeating the same toile for the wall covering and the window treatment helps to soften the angled walls and ceiling. An element of surprise—and of the modern— is added by the bright tones of the silk quilt, silk pillows, and lampshades, showing how accessories can update traditional decor.

WHIMSICAL WALLS: In the children's bedroom *(right),* a red-and-white striped wallpaper with a monkey-motif border is paired with blue-and-white striped curtains lined with yellow and red fabric, playfully evoking a circus tent. The duvet and the painted dresser continue the primary-color scheme, while the vibrant area rug features a parade of animals and performers set off against an indigo background.

COLOR INGENUITY: **CONTRAST**

A ROOM WITHOUT CONTRAST IS LIKE A LANDSCAPE ON A FOGGY DAY

Using two contrasting colors—a strong dark and a strong light—in a decorating palette provides an opportunity to create a play of shapes and patterns. Contrasting colors define a room's dimensions and establish an interesting complexity and depth.

Contrast also brightens colors and emphasizes shapes. Imagine how your room would look if photographed in black-and-white. Would the whole space soften into a range of barely distinguishable grays? Or would the space—reduced to black-and-white—become more sculptural and architectural? Would lights and darks establish interesting lines and shadows? If yes, then you have used contrast effectively to balance and shape the room.

Contrast can also take the form of a contrast of materials. The energy between a silk-covered sofa and an iron-and-glass coffee table, for example, or a mirrored bureau set on a bamboo floor, introduces another level of contrast and interest to the room.

In the living room and hall of this home, the dramatic contrast of deep blue walls and crisp white woodwork, echoed in the blue and white linen fabric, creates a strong statement. The limited use of a third color—in this case a red currant— serves as the "neutral" between dark and light that supports the effect.

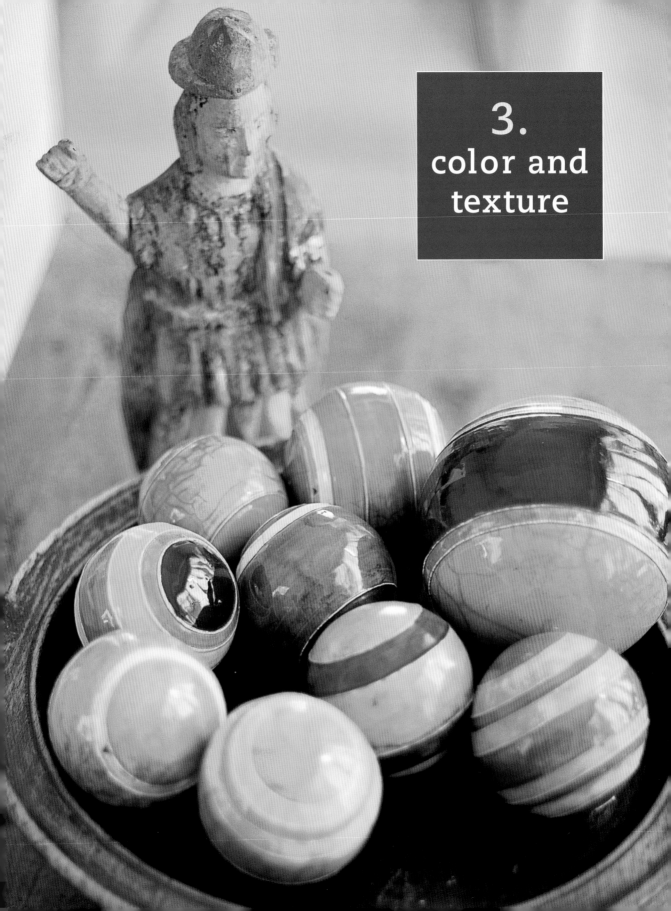

3.
color and texture

THE PROJECT: A California home brings the garden's colors into a modern house.

THE COLOR SCHEME: Curry orange, mustard yellow, lime green, lemon yellow, violet, coral, and pumpkin

THE INSPIRATION: The homeowners' long-standing love of yellows, oranges, and greens, plus the colors of the plantings around the house

WHAT WENT RIGHT: The curry-colored limestone chosen for the kitchen island established the palette for the room.

SENTIMENTAL FAVORITE: Ceramic pitchers, cups, and vases collected over the years provide color cues.

JUST FOR FUN: A vibrant still life depicting a basket of golf balls dominates a lemon yellow wall in the home office.

When Sharon and Michael Cherry began working with their interior designer and friend Gayle Mandle on a color scheme for their new house in southern California, it was clear that one color would play a big part: yellow. "We've always used a variety of yellows as a thread through every house we've owned," says Sharon

PALETTE CODE: Designed as the color code for the rest of the house, the living room incorporates paler shades of the strong hues that appear elsewhere. The walls and drapes are pale yellow, and the accent pillows on the beige sofa are lavender, light green, and soft coral. The indoor-outdoor connection is a major feature of this California house, whose backyard is framed by the living room's large windows.

Cherry. "It's Michael's favorite color, and it is the color of many objects I've collected over the years." Indeed, the color is a constant theme, from the house's soft yellow exterior right through to its putty yellow living room and lemon yellow office. Handmade yellow jugs found on the couple's travels abroad line a kitchen shelf. A painted

LOOK TO NATURE: Color inspirations include the oranges and reds of a plant in a terra-cotta container *(above)*.
DINING BY THE TERRACE: A mango and limestone palette was chosen for the dining room *(right)* to connect the space with the limestone terrace outside. An antique drop-leaf table that seats eight has a white painted finish. The fabric on the upholstered armchairs relates to the tiled floors. Colorful art appears throughout the house.

yellow armoire is a favorite bedroom piece. Even the enameled cookware on the stove is yellow. Sharon Cherry's other favorite colors—orange and green—fill the house as well.

The living room was made the palest room on purpose. "My design concept was to make the living room a bleached version of the colors in the rest of the house," says interior designer Gayle Mandle. Her reasoning was twofold. First, the living room is the biggest space in the house and one of the first rooms guests and visitors see, so she opted for restraint

COLOR-SATURATED LIBRARY: The rich purple *(above and right)* of the library's bookcases satisfies the homeowners' preference for reading amid color rather than the dark wood of a traditional library. An unexpected benefit, says Sharon Cherry, is that the purple hue is a strong link to the colors outside. "We feel as tied to the exterior in this room as we do in rooms with doors open to the outdoors," says Cherry.

and subtlety. Second, and perhaps more important, the living room has huge glass windows with views of the garden and the ocean beyond. Keeping the palette subdued allows the colors of nature to dominate.

The strongest dose of color may be found in the kitchen, whose walls and ceiling are painted a curry orange inspired by the hue of the island's limestone countertop. "I'd never had a center island in any house before," says Sharon

FAVORING CURRY: The curry hue of the limestone chosen for the island countertop *(left)* was the inspiration for the kitchen's wall and ceiling color *(above)*. One side of the island countertop features a chiseled, irregular edge that provides unexpected texture. (Before installation, the edge was buffed to remove roughness.) The cabinetry was initially supposed to be curry colored as well, but the homeowners and designer decided that might be too much of a good thing, so they opted for bleached wood instead. The stainless steel appliances strike a sleek, cool note in the otherwise spicy-hot kitchen.

ARTFUL KITCHEN: The yellow walls and cabinets showcase a collection of ceramic pots and jugs *(opposite)*. A red and yellow textile wall hanging accentuates the room's hues, as do the red ribbon chairs.

POTTERY PALETTE: A handmade ceramic jug filled with flowers *(above)* adds a fresh green accent to the kitchen.

LIGHT AND BRIGHT: Strong natural light illuminates the guest bathroom *(right)*, whose yellow palette extends from the wall color through the chair and drapery fabric to the cement floor tiles. A transparent glass sink and vanity add another texture and a reflective surface.

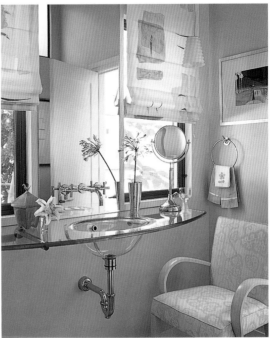

Cherry, "so I wanted this one to be really incredible." The curry is a splash of pure color amid the other, more neutral surfaces in the room: bleached wood floors and cabinets, stainless steel appliances, and countertops. The overall effect is nevertheless one of color density, in part because of the unbroken expanse of color that runs up the wall and across the ceiling.

BUTTERFLY YELLOW: A painted yellow armoire *(above)* that the homeowners found on the East Coast gives their California master bedroom a dose of color.

MOOD BOARD: The interplay of texture with Sharon Cherry's favorite colors—oranges, greens, yellows, and violets—can be seen in the mood board *(right)*.

The library is also vivid with color: The room's built-in bookcases, paneling, and ceiling are all a deep plum purple, while the rug is apricot. "We have always done our reading amid color, the way some people like to read amid lots of dark wood," notes Sharon Cherry. The sofas are covered in a terra-cotta denim.

The master bedroom's palette of green and white, with lavender accents, was chosen to invoke a sense of serenity. The walls, ceiling, and carpeting are a half-strength version of Sharon Cherry's favorite lime green. "Since we were taking the color right up to the ceiling, Gayle suggested we cut it in half, and she was absolutely right," says Cherry. Lightweight white curtains emphasize the natural light and the colors outdoors. Inside, the room's bed, chaise, and armchair are all neutral, with the omnipresent dose of yellow supplied by an armoire with a distinctive butterfly-shaped latch.

SERENE HAVEN: For the master bedroom, the home-owners and their designer chose a palette of green, white, and lavender, with the emphasis on green for its connotations of health, nature, and tranquility. They used a diluted version of their favorite shade because they wanted to paint the ceiling as well as the walls, and they felt the original strong green might be overwhelming.

While color is embraced throughout the house—in the mango walls of the dining room, the guest room's palette of pumpkin, watermelon, and lavender, and Michael's lemon yellow office—it is well balanced by neutral spaces. The master bathroom has white cabinetry and fixtures and a limestone floor the same color as the bark on the trees just outside.

"People always say this is a happy house," says Sharon Cherry, "and it's because of the light and the colors." But she also knows how much hard work went into getting those colors right. "Every wall has at least three coats of paint on it," notes Cherry, who continues to paint every surface until she's satisfied with it, no matter how many coats it takes. Explains this color aficionado, "I think there is no substitute for an absolutely beautiful color well layered on the wall."

Another secret to the success of the color scheme is Cherry's adventurous spirit. "It's the accumulated experience of living with color over a long period of time, in different houses—and having a willingness to take risks," says Cherry. Working

COLORFUL QUARTERS: The guest room's palette is playful and vibrant, with pumpkin-colored walls and ceiling, orchid-colored chairs, sage green bed pillows, and pumpkin and coral drapes. The neutral floor covering gives the eye a place to rest.

with designer and artist Gayle Mandle, who is known for her love of vibrant colors, helped Cherry decide where to have cozy colors, where to have dramatic colors, and even where to have neutrals. But it all comes back to a love of color. "I always encourage people to think about color as a best friend," advises Cherry. "Put the color you love most in

MOOD BOARD: A collection of varied fabrics and color references *(above)* shows an assortment of textures.

ORANGE BEAUTY: The guest room's orange palette *(right)* appears especially vivid when contrasted with the greenery outdoors; green and orange are two of the homeowners' favorite hues.

BRIGHT STUDY:
Lemon yellow walls,
a tomato red sofa, a
purple ottoman, and a
multicolored desk chair
make color statements
in Michael Cherry's study.
The utilitarian desk is a
simple construction of
yellow sawhorses with a
painted plywood top.

COLOR INGENUITY: COLOR AND TEXTURE

THE USE OF TEXTURE IS AS IMPORTANT AS THE CHOICE OF COLORS

Texture adds complexity and interest to a color palette. It can be visual as well as tactile. The simpler the color scheme, the more important texture becomes. And the boldest and most colorful schemes would look garish and cartoonlike if they were not tempered by a variety of textures and materials.

In decorating, when we think of texture, we think primarily of textiles. Various kinds of fabrics are suitable for upholstery and window treatments, and they are most easily divided into prints and wovens. Prints are commonly cotton, cotton blends, and linen blends. They tend to be flat and the texture subtle. Wovens are endlessly varied and include chenilles, velvets, tweeds, wools, silks, suedes, leathers, metallic novelty fabrics, natural fibers, and imitation fur, to name a few.

Textured braids, cords, and trimmings are used selectively to enhance the fabrics. Rug textures range from standard wall-to-wall pile to Orientals, woven fleece, tufted rugs, sisal, and printed floor coverings. Other materials like wood, stone, tile, mirrored surfaces, bamboo, embossed leather, metals, and glass offer their own unique surfaces.

With so many potential variables, committing to a color palette is essential. Variety is critical, but too many surfaces can be as unsettling as having too many colors in your palette. In this California home, the interior designer struck the perfect balance, using a satisfying mix of materials that take full advantage of the architecture, light, and location.

4.
color
discipline

ELLSWORTH KELLY : SCULPTURE

Three paintings in Annette Born's loft sum up her palette: each is a block of color, one red, one yellow, one blue. "I'm very interested in primary colors," says Born, a commercial real estate broker who grew up in Ohio, surrounded by the midcentury modern furniture that her parents admired. Her previous condo, however, had a very different aesthetic, one she describes as "cutesy and country." Purchasing a converted garage gave her an opportunity to return to her design roots.

"This place demanded a midcentury modern approach," says

AN EYE FOR COLOR: The oak floors and white walls of the loft's living-dining area provide an effective backdrop for Born's collections of colorful artwork and furnishings, including a Mondrianesque painting purchased at auction for just $15.

Born, now an avid collector of 1950s, '60s, and '70s furniture and pottery. Keeping the loft's bigger surfaces neutral—the nineteen-foot-high walls are white, and the solid concrete ceiling is gray—allowed her to introduce her preferred primary hues via architectural elements and colorful collections. The design and color of the custom steel railing that defines the second level of the loft were inspired by a framed print depicting a blue and white grid. The stairway's banister, also steel, is painted the same blue. A chair in the

ON THE GRID: The framed blue and white artwork on the wall of the lower level *(above)* inspired the grid design of the upper level's railing.
PRIMARY ART: The three paintings on the loft wall *(right)* tell the story of the color palette for the space. A red womb chair, a modernist furniture icon designed in 1948 by Eero Saarinen that is still in production, rests atop a French art rug.

upper-level office area is upholstered in lipstick red. The tubular metal frame of a 1970s dining chair is bright yellow.

For Born, the loft's industrial setting makes a perfect background for her many collections, because she never has to worry that the color-drenched objects will clash. She admits, "Every time I see bold color, I'm attracted to it." She succeeds in maintaining the overall look of her loft by being rigorously disciplined with regard to her passion: every-thing—all furnishings, books, and art—is consistent with her love of the midcentury modern era and her commit-ment to the use of primary colors.

DESIGN ICONS: Splashes of color are provided by the books and pottery arranged in a vintage desk by modernist designer George Nelson *(above)* and by a collection of 1950s enameled Krenit bowls *(right)*.

COLOR INGENUITY: COLOR DISCIPLINE

THE BOLDER THE COLORS, THE FEWER YOU NEED

Bold colors require courage, commitment, and control. No matter how many good ideas we have, success requires careful planning. Decorating can be a lot like shopping for clothes, and enthusiasm can fly in every direction. But the more colors you bring in, the more critical it is to maintain discipline. Some people lack any practical restraint when it comes time to shop, but multiply the folly of an extravagant shoe purchase by the cost to make over a room, and it is clear how important it is to plan within your concept and your budget.

Defining your color palette brings order to your ideas. Your core colors—aim for three to five, including accents—will be used for your big-commitment items: upholstery and wall paint. Collect references and swatches freely, but know that eventually you will have to edit, edit, edit. Just as we manage to pull together a cohesive outfit from our messy closets, so must

we make disciplined decisions about the colors of our furnishings. From the many possibilities you are considering, cut back to eight or six colors, try different combinations, then cut back again to your final three.

A firmly edited palette will allow room for changes later. You can add splashes of color in other, less permanent ways—such as accent pillows, throws, lamp shades, and collections that you can change and rearrange often to transform and freshen the look of the room. Starting with discipline and focus allows you to build a successful design.

The owner of this home had a distinctive point of view and historical design references to guide her decisions. She had the discipline to stick to her chosen palette to create a cohesive whole.

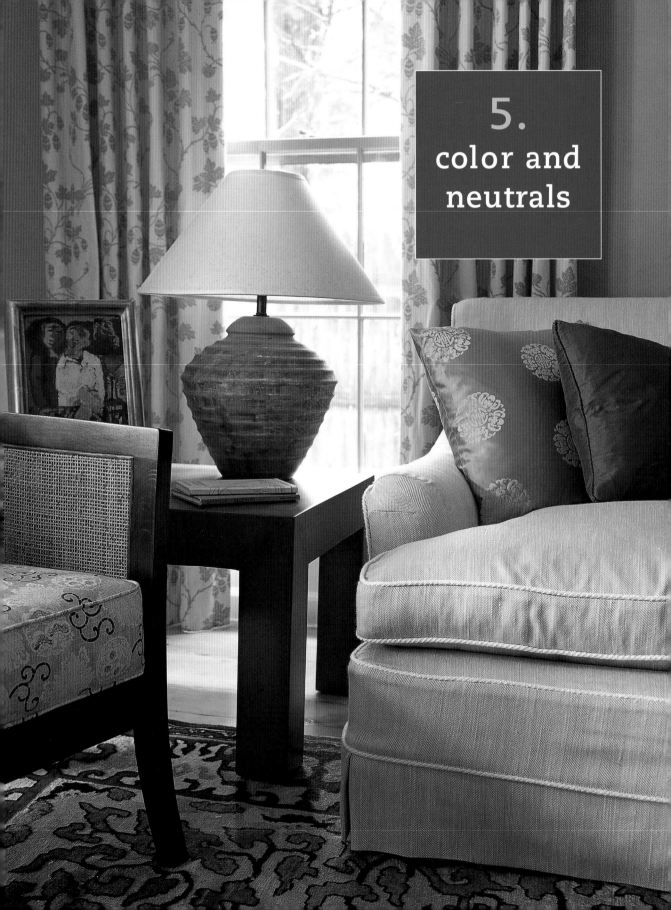

5.
color and neutrals

n the twenty-five years since Leah Robins and her husband, Leif Larsen, bought one of the oldest houses in Watertown, Massachusetts, a rambling three-story structure then in poor condition, they have remade it in their own creative likeness. Just off a busy city street, the house has over the years become surrounded by sheltering trees and hedges that make it feel surprisingly quiet and countrylike. Robins, an artist turned interior designer, and Larsen, a special-effects pro for television, have taken down walls, exposed beams, pickled

ART INSPIRED: The living room's color scheme of coral and blue was inspired by the colors of the antique Chinese rug, as well as by a set of Japanese prints elsewhere in the house. The two-tone beige draperies and a neutral sofa are restful elements against the vivid walls. Natural wood tones and a pottery lamp balance the textiles. The chair cushion and accent pillows on the sofa incorporate the unusual wall color.

floors, converted an unheated attached barn into a family room, and restored fireplaces and chimneys, all while raising their two sons, now aged seventeen and nineteen. The house, in short, has been a passion. "We've done everything ourselves, in a very eclectic way," says Robins.

Now, with the major construction finally completed, Robins is attending to the house's decoration. In this phase she is free to pursue a fascination with color that dates back to a recurring

IN A BROWN STUDY: An antique Turkish rug's traditional design *(above)* was the color inspiration for the family room, originally an attached barn. The plain sofa and striped chair are a nice pairing with the rug's medallion pattern.

STEP RIGHT IN: Robins custom-mixed one of her special colors, a subtle gray green, for the walls in the entry hall *(right)*, just inside the dark green front door. The ochre yellow French doors lead to the family room. Exposed beams, hardwood floors, and a wood console in the entryway bring in several tones of brown. The wool runner picks up both the ochre and the pale gray green and introduces splashes of coral and blue, a reference back to the palette of the living room.

dream she had as a child: "I was always dreaming that I had found a color that had never been invented," she says. "I especially love the ambiguity of color, and how it can look so different depending on the light," says Robins. With that awareness in mind, she painted the walls of her formal living room a copper coral hue that changes throughout the day. "Once I put that color on the wall, everything else needed to be calm," she says, noting that the draperies and sofa are beige. In the library across the hall, the palette has been limited to blue, white, and brown, colors drawn from the room's striped flatweave rug. "I wanted a simple room that was the baseline for the palette throughout the house," she says.

In addition to her own intrinsic love of color, Robins's color decisions were guided by the fact that the foliage around the house can cause some rooms to seem dark. "Everything I do is to warm up and lighten the rooms," she says. It's just one more factor to be considered by someone who loves to think about color.

FARMHOUSE KITCHEN: The vintage French doors leading from the kitchen's eating area to the back terrace became a focal point when painted a custom red created by homeowner Leah Robins. The bright blue chair was made by one of her sons. The Norwegian pine corner cupboard has been in her husband's family for many years. The floor is green slate.

LIGHT TOUCH: Windows were added over the kitchen sink *(above)* to bring more light into the room, which features exposed beams and cherry cabinetry. The utilitarian stainless steel sink and practical white laminate counters are accented by blue and white Dutch tiles used as a backsplash.

PAIRING OFF: In a corner of the dining room *(right)*, the blues of the dining chair seat fabric and the rug pair off with the browns of the exposed post, chair frame, and wood floor. Blue and brown appear in a variety of iterations throughout the house.

BASELINE PALETTE: The library's flatweave rug and floral sofa fabric *(opposite)* both continue the house's color message. Robins deliberately kept the room simple, leaving her options open to make additions over time.

COLOR INGENUITY: COLOR AND NEUTRALS

THE STRONGER THE COLORS, THE GREATER THE NEED TO CREATE SPACE AROUND THEM

Any use of bold color needs to be relieved with breathing space. Too much color, uninterrupted, is confusing and can even be stressful. At the other extreme, uninterrupted neutrals are dull. Neutrals—at least in my book—include any fabrics, carpets, wall coverings, or painted finishes in white, beige, or gray, as well as wood finishes in natural browns or blacks.

For example, color can be thoughtfully introduced into a fully neutral room, maintaining a serene feel but waking it up to be more creative and interesting. Likewise, a bold, colorful room will need neutral elements to bring visual order and harmony.

One or two well-chosen colors are ideal foils for a quiet room, while one or two neutrals are the perfect counterpoint for a strong one. In the appealing living room of this home, for example, a coppery wall color, soft corals, and blues fit in nicely with the natural linen upholstery and wood floor. In other rooms, the palette of cream, brown, and blue and the wood details predominate.

6.
**color
splash**

THE PROJECT: Susan and her husband repaint an all-white city apartment as a colorful refuge.
THE COLOR SCHEME: A rainbow of greens, yellows, pinks, violet, plum, and lavender
THE INSPIRATION: A love of vivid patterns, colors, and environments
WHAT WENT RIGHT: Passageways became focal points with the addition of decorative painted murals.
BOLDEST MOVE: A hall mural that rocks
JUST FOR FUN: The four-story staircase has nine different shades of pale blue.

Behind the front doors of many residences in Boston's Beacon Hill neighborhood can be found somber, luxurious furnishings, collections of good antiques, and fine paintings. Other buildings are home to students and renters whose Ikea furniture is placed beside marble fireplaces and floor-to-ceiling windows. All of them are imbued with the history of one of the oldest cities in America.

For my husband and me, the opportunity to establish ourselves in a vertical slice of townhouse was

HELLO SUNSHINE: In the kitchen, located three steps below street level, a cheerful palette of greens and yellows turns a basement space into a sunny garden. The color scheme was based on the fabric used for the window shade. The island and cabinet brackets are accentuated with a strong lime green paint.

irresistible. The four stories—one room wide and two rooms deep—had been nicely restored by a former architect-owner. But it was—to my admittedly color-obsessed eye—a boringly blank slate. When we first saw it, walls, furniture, and paneling were unrelentingly white. The house needed to work for our own tastes, and repainting was clearly in order, top to bottom, in the appealing colors that we thrive on. A color palette was developed for each floor, considering the architectural features, the light, and the room's use. To connect the floors, the entire staircase wall was painted in a sequence of pale blues. The passageways—small halls—on each level were

GEOMETRY: The three interior steps up to street level from the kitchen *(above)* have been incorporated in a corner where inventive use of space and ingenious custom woodwork make every inch count.

MOOD BOARD: A floral fabric *(opposite)* was the color inspiration for the kitchen, which includes three yellow and two green shades of paint.

designated "art walls" and scheduled for decorative painting. Although still a work-in-progress, the house today has over forty colors and is both exhilarating and homey.

On the lowest level, a few steps below the street, a small side door opens directly into the kitchen. The layout of the kitchen's cabinets and paneling, designed by the former architect-owner, is both creative and astoundingly functional, making the utmost use of the small space. Storage is provided by a mix of open shelving and cabinets with both glass-fronted and raised-panel doors. The variations provided a wonderful series of panels, planes, and moldings on which to conduct an exciting color experiment.

The kitchen color scheme was inspired by a fabric in various yellows and greens. The fabric picked up on several color

URBAN AND ELEGANT: The dining room colors *(right)* were chosen to work around a floral fabric in blues, greens, and grays. Lavender walls, pale green trim, and two shades of gray establish the paint assortment. Bright lime paint picks out the mantelpiece for a surprising twist.

elements that were already in place: the limestone floor was dark green, the counter-tops were a warm mahogany, the appliances were stainless steel, and the backsplash tiles were (of course) white. Ultimately, four shades of yellow were selected for the cabinets and walls. Lemony shades brighten the paneling on the cabi-nets, while a darker apricot defines the bead that accents them. Two lime greens were used: a paler tone for the glass-fronted cup-boards, and a deeper one for the island brackets, chair rail, and baseboards.

The passageway between the kitchen and the dining room can be seen from both rooms. Because the exuberant kitchen evokes a very dif-ferent mood than the more sedate dining room, the hall wall colors were chosen to unify the two spaces and soften the transi-tion between them. We hand-painted the "wallpaper" (*above*) starting with a sage ground color related to the dining room's palette. The floral elements pick up the colors used on the kitchen cabinetry.

The lavender-walled dining room opens onto a pocket-handkerchief-

MAKING COLOR ARRANGEMENTS: An unconven-tional symmetry is achieved with a grouping of artwork, objects, and floor lamps against a lavender wall in the dining room. The striped drum lampshades flank the narrow console table, which is scaled for the small city dining room.

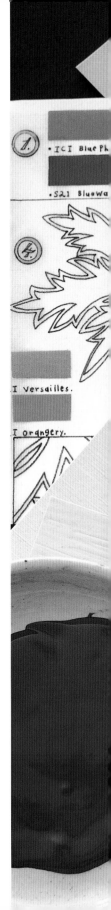

sized back garden. Here again, clever cabinetry issued an invitation to experiment with the use of multiple shades of a single color. The paneling is picked out in three shades of café au lait, emphasizing the shadows cast by the moldings. The trim and the French doors are painted a pale gray green. The overall effect is integrated by a floral fabric used for the curtains, which repeats the color story. Two shades of bright green are used as surprising accents on the fireplace woodwork.

Three steps up from the street, the front door opens into the hall, with the library on the left and the living room straight ahead. A vivid mural was painted on the long wall

SPLASH: The hallway mural *(above and overleaf)* was painted by Maine artist Matt Cote, who has made a name for himself painting rooms and walls in his own inventive style (his tools of the trade are shown at right). He collaborates with clients on designs and colors, giving thoughtful attention to scale, transition, and the experience of the final work. Once the design is approved, Matt lays out the lines of the design and then paints freehand in oils. His art form revives a long tradition of murals by itinerant painters who traveled New England in the nineteenth century as decorative artists.

BOOKING IT: The built-in bookcases and paneling in the library take on a new look in vibrant green paint; the backing for the bookcases is a pale lavender blue. A comfortable armchair has a large-scale pattern and a distinctive texture.

facing the stairs by a young painter, whom I collaborated with on the design. Visible from the library, the living room, and the staircase, the mural glows and shimmers at the heart of the house.

In the library, paneled walls and bookcase doors take center stage: they are painted vivid green, set off by the insides of the bookcases, which are a pale shade of the lavender blue wall color. An upholstered armchair gives the room

MOOD BOARD: The startlingly vivid lime woodwork of the library bookcases evokes the freshness of leaves.

LIGHT PASSAGE: The tiny hallway between the library and the mango living room *(right)* includes built-in bookcases painted high-gloss white, a match for the doorway trim. Transoms above the doorways help disperse light throughout the first floor.

a dose of pink, the third element in a green-blue-pink palette. The glossy white crown molding, window and door trim, add a crisp contrast to the vibrant colors.

The living room's main color feature is the rich yellow gold of its walls. Used mainly in the evening, this space was given a warm palette of yellow, orange, and fuchsia to foster a mood conducive to conversation. The walls are complemented by a pale yellow ceiling. All of the woodwork was painted with a high-gloss oil paint that makes it shine beautifully in sunlight or lamplight. The long striped curtains are made from a Swedish fabric.

In the master suite, which comprises the third level, each room tells a compelling color story. The bedroom's two-hue palette is established by its larger surfaces: the walls and paneling are painted in a mix of pale gray green and

BRIGHT CONVERSATION: The welcoming living room, with its mango orange walls, deep orange sofa, and fuchsia armchairs, is the warm center of the house, sunny by day and warmly lit by night. Simple striped draperies accentuate the tall windows. All of the trim was painted in a high-gloss white that bounces back the light from the tall windows. In a change from the usual white, the ceiling color here is pale yellow, about 10 percent of the wall tone, to reflect a soft golden light into the room.

teal. Gauzy sheer curtains trimmed with pink ribbon and a variety of other pink textiles playfully accent the cooler colors.

The master bathroom featured lots of marble, whose gray veining directed how much and what color could be added. Three shades of gray were chosen for the woodwork, and a rich violet-blue was selected for the walls. The passageway between the bedroom and bathroom has built-in closets and drawers; future plans call for a design to be stenciled on the long wall.

SUITE PINK: The master bedroom *(left)* has airy sheer silk curtains and a color palette of gray green and rose. The paneling and walls are painted a very pale eucalyptus green in three shades of varying intensity, with teal accents on the woodwork, as shown in the mood board *(above)*.

SETTLE IN: The all-marble bath-room felt like one in a good hotel but lacked personality. Bright violet walls make every bath a calming experience. The lavender gray paint shades used on the cabinets and woodwork match the veining in the marble.

The two rooms on the top floor are used as a home office and a guestroom. A skylight is positioned over the staircase, and though the office walls are a vintage-feeling green, the archway presented a perfect opportunity to introduce another color. The high-gloss plum paint adds a defining accent.

MOOD BOARD: Here, several shades of vintage green partner with light and dark plum. An old platter inspired the color combination.

MAKING AN ENTRANCE: The office on the top floor *(opposite)* has a plum doorway picked out in high-gloss paint and a soft pale green window trim and baseboards.

COLOR INGENUITY: COLOR SPLASH

THE MORE
AMBITIOUS THE
COLOR PALETTE,
THE MORE
IMPORTANT THE
METHOD TO
YOUR MADNESS

Warning: Color is addictive. We all have intensely personal responses to color, and there are as many tastes as there are people. I—and fortunately my family—choose to live in rooms awash with color—the more, the better. Getting it the way you want it requires many steps:

• Always look at colors in daylight for a full spectrum, and also check them at night in incandescent (yellow) light to see if they hold.

• Consider colors in the context of the room's architecture: existing components like woodwork, flooring, and available light.

• Plan your palette with extra care when using bold colors.

• Keep color values equal. If you commit to brights, don't add a muddy color into the mix. If you need a break, use white or black or a different shade of the same color.

• Make proportions unequal. One color should dominate and be used in more than one variation. The second color should be used in moderation, and the third only lightly.

• Keep it simple. Strong colors do not need a lot of textures, trims, swags, and fussy styling to be interesting, unlike white and beige.

• Strong colors should not fight or overpower each other. Contrast heightens the colors, and when combined with others, colors take on a different personality.

• Extreme color should be used in limited doses. A wild mural should be balanced with a plain floor. One bright room should open into the next with a break or a quiet link in between.

7.
color families

It takes only a few moments of conversation with Christine Miles to realize that her approach to color is 100 percent emotional. "I don't really have one color scheme; I change frequently," she says. "For each room, I think in terms of how you want to feel in that room. What are the three adjectives? Then I choose the colors."

Among her upbeat choices are a vibrant green for the kitchen; red, orange, and green for the family room; and blue and coral for her sitting room/home office. These are dynamic colors, well suited to a household that includes Christine, her husband Josiah, and three children aged six, eleven, and twelve. The palettes also speak to

COMFORT COLORS: A favorite color combination—coral and turquoise—transforms a small room into Christine's personal haven.

an ease with color that comes naturally to one whose family business is a well-known local building-supply house, with a popular paint and decorating center.

Christine calls her choices "feel-good colors," a description that became a reality one holiday vacation when every member of the family came down with the flu. Their cure?

MAKE A CONNECTION: A wall of built-in shelving in the family room *(above)*, a recent addition to the 1850s house, displays favorite objects and books. The interior is painted in alternating colors—two shades of green, a red, and an orange—and provides a visual link to the red and green kitchen, which is adjacent.

COLOR MUST-HAVES: Red leather chairs surround the kitchen table *(right)*, providing a burst of color. The black hutch is Christine's response to the design truism that dictates that every room must always include a little bit of black.

"We each painted a few strokes on the kitchen barstools," says Christine. "It lifted our spirits."

In addition to considering the emotional impact of color, Christine pays attention to connections from room to room. "I always think about the next few rooms you can see and make sure there is something connecting them by color," she says. For example, the cheerful green of the kitchen walls is repeated around the corner in the family room's shelving unit. Red chairs have a role in both spaces as well. "Color is definitely a passion for us," she says.

BOLD CHOICE: The children chose the colors for their bedrooms. Vibrant orange *(left)* was twelve-year-old Henry's pick, chosen from a sample book. An interesting plaid valance is partnered with a shade in the same material. Laying out fabrics and colorful household objects *(above)* is one way to play with possibilities.

BLUE VIOLET TREND: Eleven-year-old Francis was adamant about having a very bright blue on the walls of his room *(above)*. Violet and lavender fabrics enhance the effect and witness the current increase in popularity of all shades of purple.

MOOD BOARD: An assemblage of beads, glass, and fabrics *(right)* creates a family of blue.

COLOR INGENUITY: COLOR FAMILIES

In the 1930s, dye expert and colorist Albert Munsell identified three color characteristics: *hue*, the color family; *value*, the lightness or darkness; and *color*, the range of tonal and chromatic values. Working within one color family provides an opportunity to use various light and dark, delicate and saturated shades of a single color. The chosen color family can shift within a room, or it can extend through a series of rooms.

The goal of this approach is not a sweater-set look, where everything is an exact match. Variety of tone, texture, and contrast is essential—and more critical than when a broader color range is used. Neutrals like white and wood should be incorporated. Consider how the colors interact, and take care to adjust them when necessary. For instance, all blues are not created equal. An electric royal blue looks confusing next to a

subdued dusky blue. A pair of dark and light bright blues
would be better companions, as would two soft dusky ones.

Francis's bedroom features at least nine different colors
from the blue family. The values range across extremes: a
deep violet rug and deep blue green walls juxtaposed with
pale blue embroidered details on the bedding and an airy
organic motif on the linen curtains. The variety of materials—cotton bedding, wool rug, matte paint, and crewelwork
on linen—demonstrates how specific the color direction was
and how interesting it became. Color families can also be
defined more loosely, as in the citrus family chosen for the
orange bedroom, but should always support each other in
meaningful ways.

8.
color
traditions

As color inspirations go, few could get more personal than the one that guided architect Ramsay Gourd and his wife, interior designer Mary Jo Gourd. Throughout their 1820s Colonial house, in Manchester Village, Vermont, hang paintings done by Ramsay's grandfather, a society portrait painter in the 1920s. The colors of those portraits spoke to the couple like an interesting whisper from the past. "We chose the wall color for the dining

PAST PERFECT: New colors—celadon walls, aubergine woodwork—enhance the play of light and dark in this Colonial-era dining room. A vivid rug adds vibrance to the bright countenance of the room.

room from the celadon that is in a portrait of Ramsay's grandmother, done by his grandfather," says Mary Jo. Once they selected a dominant color, the Gourds relied on their own creative sensibilities to expand the palette. In the dining room, for example, they picked aubergine to complement the celadon walls, but only after some trial and error with an overly bright shade of purple that Mary Jo likes to call "Barney" purple. The other rooms evolved in a similar fashion, colors chosen for sentimental reasons juxtaposed with hues that suited the family's modern-day life.

LOOKING IN: Two tones of yellow enliven the walls of the family room *(above)* and distinguish it from the adjacent formal dining room.
SUPPORT THE PALETTE: Colored glass vases *(right)* catch the light that filters into the dining room and echo the celadon and aubergine palette.

The kitchen features a healthy dose of red, a family favorite. The master bathroom's scheme of sky blue and springtime green was inspired by a small painting of flowers in bloom in Vermont during July, the month the Gourds were married. And Ramsay's interest in painted patterns led to the choice of two shades of yellow in a diamond motif on the family-room walls. End result: a house cheerful enough to make an ancestral portrait smile.

FAMILY AFFAIR: Setting a table with brightly colored linens *(above)* is a perfect way to introduce color in an eating area. Here, nature's harmony guides the colorful arrangement: the plate and tablecloth mimic the green of a Granny Smith apple, while the napkin is printed with random dots of petal red. Yellow walls and plank ceilings *(right)* give the family room a rustic, casual air, a homey backdrop for casual meals.

PAINT A PATTERN: In the family room *(above)* a harlequin pattern adds a playful element to the walls and provides a neutral backdrop for a collection of metal stars in weathered tones of red and green.

PERSONAL CHECK: The checkerboard floor that enlivens the kitchen *(right)* was handpainted by homeowner Ramsay Gourd. He pickled the wood floor first, then painted the black and white squares. The red and black kitchen cabinetry was chosen in part because the family previously had lived in an all-white kitchen—and wanted something livelier and more fun.

BRIGHT ENTRY: The Gourds wanted their entry hall *(opposite)* to make a bright first impression so they based its colors on the pottery displayed in a painted cabinet visible at the far end of the space. Blues and greens, accented by the white of the trim and ceiling, now greet family and visitors as they come through the door.

PRETTY BEDROOM: In a guest bedroom *(above)*, the walls are painted a robin's-egg blue, and the bed linens are lime green and periwinkle, a color scheme that creates a restful atmosphere for sleeping and relaxing.

INSPIRED BY NATURE: The sky blue ceiling of the master bathroom *(right)* illustrates a recent trend: ceilings are being painted to match the wall color, to contrast with it using a lighter or darker shade, or in another color altogether. This formerly overlooked area offers an ideal opportunity for a defining color treatment.

COLOR INGENUITY: **COLOR TRADITIONS**

TRADITIONAL
INTERIORS NEED
NOT BE BOUND
BY NARROW
COLOR CHOICES

There is often a fear of bringing new colors into the traditional world of Oriental rugs and dark dining rooms. Owning nice antiques should not dissuade you from making a color update. Good Oriental rugs contain many colors—at least one of which you can highlight and elaborate on. Antique furniture has a lovely patina and is only enhanced when placed in more colorful surroundings. Fortunately, today's flexible design approach encourages the use of creative colors to enliven and modernize older homes.

Choosing colors for a traditional home is about harmony. Whether the palette is bold and bright or soft and luminous, the color groupings must complement the smaller rooms and

fine woodwork. Avoid primary colors, as they are generally too simple and harsh. Strong colors should not overpower weaker ones. Vivid accent colors should be used in smaller doses. As you build your palette, consider adding a little gray or beige to soften brighter colors.

The selection of colors needs to be appropriate for the context of the room. The aubergine woodwork in the Gourds' dining room avoids being too purple: it is a shade both saturated and subdued. The clear celadon walls, while bright, are tempered somewhat and avoid what might have been a jarring lime. The contrast of dark woodwork and light walls conforms to tradition, but with a color twist.

slack

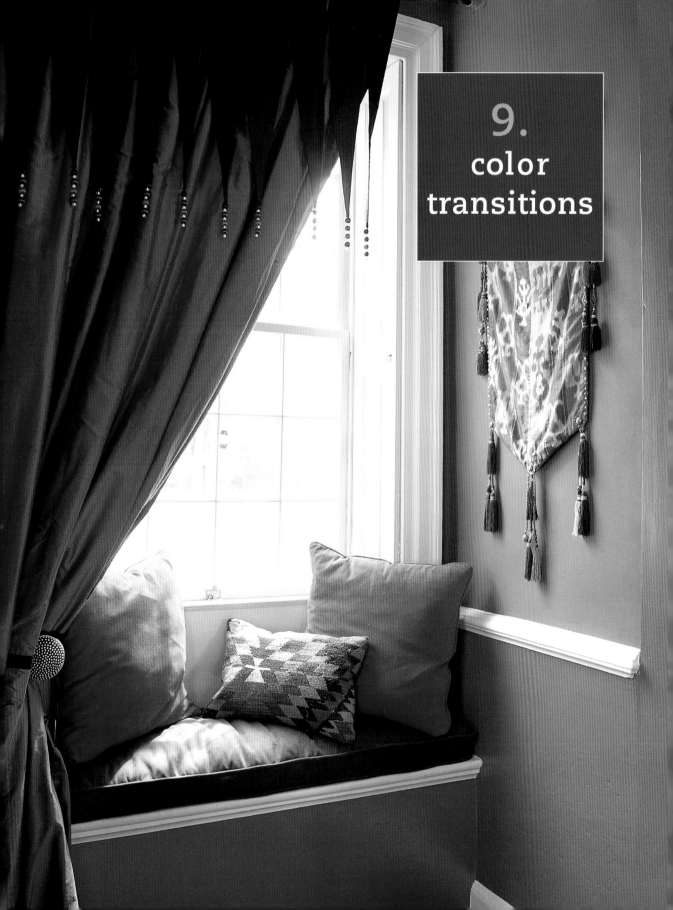

For Nancy Traversy, decorating a house is a lot like designing a book. "You want flow from room to room—or chapter to chapter—and you also need to give attention to details," says Traversy, who happens to know

HARLEQUIN AFFAIR: In the dining room, red and plum are paired with celery and black, made all the more fun by the recurring diamond motif in the rug, chair backs, and drapery valance. The suedelike fabric that covers the dining room chairs mixes colors. The ivory chair rail acts as a buffer between the plum upper wall and the red below. The drapery at the dining room's window nook *(previous page)* includes plum and red tassels accented with beads.

a lot about both endeavors. The owner of Barefoot Books, a publisher of children's titles with a cross-cultural theme, she also masterminded the design of the house she shares with her husband, Martin Lueck, and their four children, aged nine to fourteen.

When they first bought the historic house, it was a warren of rooms with outdated mechanical systems, decorated in an authentic eighteenth-century style that, while lovely, was worlds away from this family's modern and energetic life. But they saw the potential and undertook an extensive renovation, opening up spaces and adding new windows

TOGETHERNESS: In today's world, many children come home from school and retreat to their rooms for homework or television. The family, determined to avoid this type of isolation, created a large family area *(above)* and kitchen *(right)* with back-to-back fireplaces and different spots for reading, snacking, snuggling, homework, and computer time. The palette of celery, red, gold, and green links all corners of what were formerly three rooms and a porch. Beyond the kitchen, the formal purple dining room makes use of the same red and celery for a logical transition.

while preserving the high ceilings and appealing quirkiness of the building.

Traversy plunged into the decorating with gusto. Inspired by the illustrations and design of the books she publishes, as well as a longtime love of fabrics, she developed a palette for the house after a week spent gathering swatches from textile shops in London. The palette's leading color is celery, which is used in every room in various shades and paired with an inspired assortment of secondary colors. The other colors in the palette—golds, plums, reds, and teals—leapfrog through the house, with celery as the constant; the colors appear not only on painted walls, but also as bold draperies pieced together from a mix of fabrics.

"I made sure there was a link in color from one room to the next," says Traversy, who, during the planning stages, kept a notebook with detailed descriptions of the fabric and paint choices for each room and spreadsheets with separate entries for walls, ceiling, baseboards, window trim, floors, and doors. Then she specified light or dark colors for each element. She made adjustments throughout the house as

COME AND EAT: Taking down the wall to a former sunporch made a nook for the family dining table, a few steps lower than the kitchen itself. The walls are red, a color thought to stimulate both conversation and appetite. The room's French doors overlook the garden.

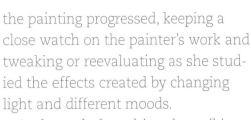

the painting progressed, keeping a close watch on the painter's work and tweaking or reevaluating as she studied the effects created by changing light and different moods.

In the end, she achieved a striking variety of moods in all the spaces where she used celery green. These rooms serve as a fascinating example of how different a particular color can look depending on what other colors it is placed next to. In the living room, for example, pale celery—in two shades—is paired with black, for an effect that is subdued and restful. Step out into the hall, and celery again meets black in the checkerboard floor. Now the strong lime woodwork becomes celery's more energetic partner. Just across the hall in the library, pale celery walls are accented with teal and black. In the kitchen, celery appears with warm reds and golds and is once again transformed. The result is a house whose vivid palette is as fanciful as a storybook's, yet sophisticated and elegant as well.

NEUTRAL ZONE: The colors in the living room were deliberately limited to celery, black, and plum—with light trim—to promote a sense of calm, because Nancy believed it was important to have an oasis within such an active household. Her four children refer to it as the "chill-out room."

TEAL APPEAL: An assortment of bottles brought back from South Africa *(above)* comprises a blue-green color mix. The palette for the library, used by Martin Lueck as a home office *(right),* is teal, celery, and black, as seen in the custom wool rug. The rug's pattern and color connect the room to the checkerboard floor just outside the door. The room has old-house architectural features that the homeowners cherish, including twelve-foot-high ceilings and window seats. Cushions and pillows in shades of green and blue set off the two-tone walls.

MOOD BOARD: The mood board *(above)* shows how the guest room's color palette and materials work together, a good example of the benefit of having a plan.

GUEST QUARTERS: A ceramic lamp and bowl in blues and greens were the color inspiration for the guest room *(right)*. The walls are painted a hue that Nancy calls duck's-egg blue. The custom-designed rug incorporates all of the colors in the room's palette.

COLOR INGENUITY: **COLOR TRANSITIONS**

**USE COLOR TO
ESTABLISH A VISUAL
CONNECTION
FROM ONE SPACE
TO ANOTHER BY
REPEATING
OR EVOLVING IT**

Whether you map out the entire color scheme for your house all at once or work room by room, you can use color to link spaces and make sense of the whole. Using color for transitions is especially useful in a house having many rooms and many strong colors, where stepping from one distinctive color scheme to the next may feel jarring. Using one color consistently eases the transition.

In this home, the transition color is a pale celery, which dances throughout the house, finding a new partner in each room. In the living room, celery is paired with black and plum, the effect subdued and elegant. In the library, it joins teal and black. The dining room's vibrant red and purple are

calmed by the celery doors and woodwork, while in the adjacent kitchen, celery cabinets mingle with warm reds and golds. The layout of this house allows for long views that can sometimes encompass three rooms at a time. The unwavering celery holds it all together.

Hallways are literal and visual transition zones. A hall that connects two mild-colored rooms might be an opportunity for a bold splash of color. Anything goes, as long as the choice provides a pleasing link between the adjacent color schemes. Between strong-colored rooms, the hall can be quiet, a peaceful pause between two compelling environments, or it can take cues from each to form a visual bridge.

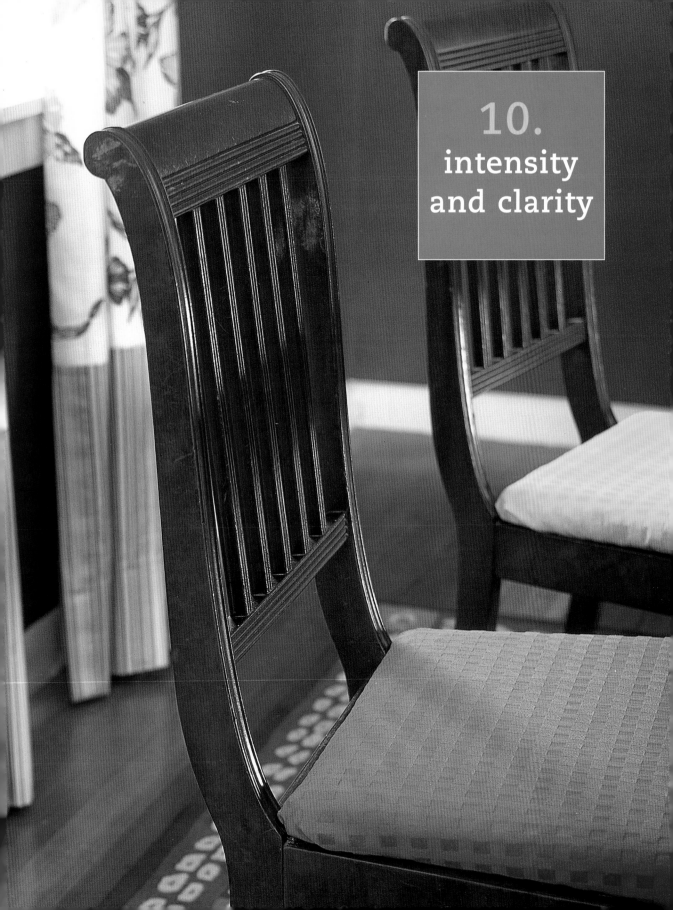

10.
intensity and clarity

There are no pastels or muted colors in the house that Beth and Bill Eyre share with their two young children, six-year-old Ramsay and three-year-old Chapin. "We feel happy being surrounded by color," says Beth. Their bold palette developed room by room.

"There were a lot of dark colors and patterned wallpapers in the house when we bought it," recalls Beth. The couple spent an entire

OPPOSITES ATTRACT: Using two colors that are opposites on the color wheel—red for the dining room and green for the bar area—creates a lively interplay. The bar area also serves as a visual transition to the sunny yellow living room. The colorful seat cushions on the dining room chairs are reminders of the palette used throughout the house.

year removing wallpaper before they started to paint. Before long, the dining room was a rich tomato red, a bathroom was vivid eggplant purple, the mudroom was brick orange, and one son's room was periwinkle blue.

When the time came to renovate the kitchen, they chose not just one color but four: Dresden blue for two walls, grass green and buttermilk yellow for the cabinets, and

MOOD BOARD: A collection of elements in various shades of yellow, orange, and green *(above)* makes it easier to visualize the final mix.
DESIGN SOLUTION: A yellow couch, with throw pillows in tones of yellow and orange and placed against a yellow wall *(right)*, is accented by a spicy rug in burnt orange and sage greens.

royal blue for the island. "Bill sometimes suspects that I choose these primary colors because I miss being in the classroom," says Beth. "But he loves every color—I start painting the walls, and he always finishes."

Throughout the house, there is none of the timidity and tentativeness that often derail a color scheme. The Eyres picked their colors and stuck to them in all their undiluted glory: dark green, royal blue, and tomato red were all used at 100 percent strength. The dining-room rug and curtains use red, blue, and green as the core colors. The back hall echoes the hot, orangey red and multicolored accents used in the dining room.

VIVID PATTERNS: The kitchen's mix of patterns and colors *(left)* is shown in the mood board *(above)*, which includes swatches of fabric, as well as color chips for the cabinetry.

The custom kitchen cabinets in blue, green, and pale yellow are paired with the strong red walls in the dining room on one side and the back-entry mudroom on the other. Taken as a whole, the primary color story is a lively representation of the family. "We love color. It's a good way to express who we are," says Beth Eyre. This personal expression takes time, though, and Beth's experience with choosing

NATURE'S BOUNTY: Fruit and flowers *(above)* bring even more color to the kitchen table, where a vibrant curtain, tablecloth, and plates set a cheerful tone.

RECIPE FOR COLOR: Inspired by the colors of the Italian pottery they use every day, the Eyres custom ordered cabinets in three different colors *(right)*. White space is provided by white walls, the glass-fronted wall cabinets, and plain countertops.

the living-room color is a telling example. Because the room has a sixteen-foot wall of windows, Beth struggled to find the perfect shade of yellow. "Yellows are so affected by sunlight that I had to keep trying new ones," she recalls. Finally, after painting test patches of six shades of yellow, the right one emerged.

FABRIC STATEMENT: The easiest way to make a quick bathroom fix is with a bright shower curtain and mat *(above)*. This plain white guest bathroom has undergone a change of mood with this vibrant scheme.
OUTDOOR DELIGHT: Ready to host a summer lunch, a table on the front porch *(right)* wears a floral cloth whose green seems to have been borrowed from the grass.

MOOD BOARD: This collage *(opposite)* shows how elements of a room can be put together during the planning stage.

YOUNG BLUE: This nursery room is filled with lively children's fabrics in assorted prints *(above and right)*. The beach scene over the bed was painted by Ramsay Eyre, age six.

VROOM ROOM: Ramsay chose green for his room *(above)*, which boasts an all-boy truck-motif area rug and a paper sun from his mom's teaching days.

CRISP WHITE TRIM: The Eyres chose terra-cotta, a warm, welcoming color, for their mudroom *(opposite)*, the first area the children see on their way inside after outdoor adventures. The bead board ceiling, peg hook rails, and door and window trim are all painted a crisp white, as is the molding and trim throughout the house. "We love the contrast of white trim against all the colors," says Beth Eyre.

COLOR INGENUITY: INTENSITY AND CLARITY

THE SATURATION AND BRILLIANCE OF COLORS INFORM THE WAY THEY ARE USED

A color is identified not only by hue and shade but also by its intensity (saturation) and clarity (brilliance). Shifts up or down the scale result in "front- seat" colors that are sharp and clear or "backseat" colors that are more understated and restrained.

A single color can appear in many different guises depending on its level of intensity and saturation. *Saturation* refers to the depth of the color: dark and intense, or light and delicate. One way to think about clarity is to think about complexity. A clear glass of apple juice becomes opaque when a little orange juice is added. Decorating is similar. You may choose a yellow that is sunny and bright for one area, while in another you opt for a more laid-back yellow with hints of brown. A clear color is made up of only a few

pigments, while a more subtle one consists of various tints. Beware, however, of undecided and muddy shades.

Brilliant and soft colors all have their merits, but it can be difficult to use them together. Clearer colors may be more appropriate for brighter, more contemporary locations, while less edgy colors will enhance traditional styles. The ideal intensity and saturation varies depending on location and mood.

The home of the Eyres demonstrates a high level of color intensity and clarity. The dining room's vibrant red walls, the kitchen's rich blues and greens, and the living room's mix of yellows stand forth loud and clear. This is color and purpose at its most direct.

THE PROJECT: Scandinavian style is the inspiration for a Nordic kitchen makeover.

THE COLOR SCHEME: Nordic grays and blues

THE INSPIRATION: The colors of the old painted furniture that Susan Sargent admired while living in Sweden

WHAT WENT RIGHT: Painting the ceiling midnight blue, between the original exposed beams, added color interest over the living and dining areas.

DESIGN DETAIL: The diamond motif on the closet doors in the entry hall links the space to the kitchen, whose cabinetry features raised diamond panels.

JUST FOR FUN: Painting the bead board wainscot of the entry hall bright green evokes a sense of springtime no matter what the season may be.

The ground floor of our pre–Civil War farmhouse in the country retains little of its past. A fire in the early 1900s gutted it, and a renovation as a ski house in the 1960s embarrassed it. (If I say that all the walls were clad in rough barn board and that the guest powder room was disguised as an outdoor privy, complete with a cutout moon in the

OPENING UP: A palette of Nordic grays and blues unifies the newly remodeled ground floor. This view from the kitchen island takes in a seating area and a fireplace with panels that match the kitchen cabinets. The ceiling between the original beams was painted blue above the seating and dining areas and left white over the kitchen work space.

door, you'll get the general idea.) The old windows were
long gone. The front door had been clapboarded over, and
the front elevation was marred by a trio of misplaced and
outsized picture windows. Inside, the staircase had been
reversed, and most of the flooring replaced with painted
plywood and stained pine. Still, the house sat on an
incredible piece of land, the frame and beams were original, and the house had its own pleasant scale and history.

Over the last twelve years, my husband and I have restored

WATCHFUL EYE: A 1920s painting, *Blue Girl (above)*, by Margarett Sargent
(Susan's great-aunt), keeps an eye on dining-room behavior.
BY THE FIRE: A single wall behind a country hutch is painted blue green as
an accent *(right)*. The flooring is beech recycled from a New England mill.

the outer shell, where properly sized and spaced windows now define the facade, in accordance with an 1890 photograph of the house in its prime. We replaced the porch and the front door and then began to adapt the rooms, one by one, for our life with two sons. The kitchen and dining room posed the biggest challenges. Early on, we had added a walk-in pantry and swapped the barn-board cabinet doors for plain fronts. But the reinstalled front door opened awkwardly into what had become the dining room, and a side door opened from the porch directly into the middle of the kitchen, leaving no place to hang coats or stow boots. Unable to find a good solution to the many problems of layout and design, we had put off until last the major renovation we knew we wanted.

Our decision to open up the dining room to the kitchen and to replace a bulky corner fireplace with a new, centrally located one was the turning point. We could now realign the kitchen by moving the sink and counters out of their dark corner and over to the west windows, which in turn

DINNER INTERLUDE: The dining room also functions as a library, with floor-to-ceiling bookshelves on the back side of the fireplace wall. A transom window brings light from the entry hall into the dining room. The chairs are classic Swedish, painted in the same shades as the walls.

allowed us to add an island and create a seating area in front of the new fireplace. The dining room/library became an active part of the kitchen, instead of a room that we seldom entered except to shelve more books. As we opened up the west wall of the dining room into the kitchen, we simultaneously shrank the space at the northern end and put up a wall that gave us a proper foyer inside the front door.

In considering how to decorate the space, I thought of the years I spent in Sweden, where I had fallen in love with the pale, gray blue tones of older furniture and walls. My palette

COLORFUL COOKING: The working kitchen *(right)* features a brushed metal and glass chandelier, an island, and limestone countertops. Raised diamond panels on the base of the island were inspired by traditional designs Susan admired while living in Sweden. The blue green paint and handmade tile on the window wall (see close-up in mood board, *above*) delineate the space dedicated to cooking.

for the new space would build off that color concept, but it would also include some nontraditional color accents. The cabinets were designed with the traditional raised-diamond panel doors often seen on Scandinavian cupboards. These, the walls, and the other woodwork were all painted in various tones of Nordic gray. To diversify the grays, a mix of materials was used for the floors: mottled blue ceramic tile for the entry hall, rough marble for the dining room, and recycled wooden factory flooring for the central part of the kitchen. The original dark beams complemented the flooring.

To add accent colors and to keep the space from seeming too monochromatic, I painted the ceiling panels between the beams a midnight blue over the seating area and the dining room. Two teal walls face each other across the working part of the kitchen. The entry hall has a different palette, a soft eucalyptus green in two shades and vivid lime wainscoting four feet high. Pairs of

LIGHT WORK: Locating the sink and counters along a western wall of windows created a light-filled work area. The cabinets were custom made to Susan's specifications by a Vermont woodworker, and the tiles over the bright blue Aga stove were made by two Rhode Island artists.

raised-diamond panels, like those in the kitchen, adorn the closet doors in the new foyer.

The most inviting aspect of all is the fireplace in the middle of the room, with its comfortable seating area in blues and grays. On one side is a large open hutch filled with pottery, books, and a stereo. Behind the fireplace, facing into the dining room, are more bookshelves. By way of its size and placement, the fireplace gives shape to the room, establishing a boundary for various functions—cooking and casual meals by the fire or more formal meals in the dining room.

READING IN BED: The downstairs guest room *(left),* reserved for Susan's mother, inherited a long bookshelf on one wall when the dining room/library was remodeled. The paneled walls were painted a soft pink, the trim and bookcase a smoky green, and the bookcase interior a glowing magenta.

POWDER-ROOM PIZZAZZ: Handprinted wallpaper in shades of blue enlivens the walls of the downstairs powder room *(above);* teal woodwork offers a restful counterpoint.

COLOR INGENUITY: **COLOR PARTNERS**

PAIRING TWO COLORS CREATES A STRONG DESIGN FRAMEWORK

There are compelling advantages to using a palette of just two colors. Committing to one dark and one light color is easy. Each color interacts with the ones around it, so having only two to tweak simplifies things considerably. It gets the "heavy lifting" out of the way, making front-end decisions more straightforward. And the color story is simple enough that add-ons, in the form of accents and accessories, can totally change the feel.

This reconfigured space combined kitchen, dining room, and seating area. Original beams, wood floor, and multiple doorways and windows made the architecture busy, even before color. The wood panels for the kitchen cabinets, island, and fireplace are based on a traditional Scandinavian raised-diamond design. The color combination of pale gray and Nordic blue unifies and simplifies the space.

The light color partner—delicate gray blue—was used in several iterations: pale on the cabinets and woodwork, and slightly darker on the dining-room walls. The ceiling, chairs, and rug in the seating area are all different values of dark blue. The kitchen, with its many windows, is predominantly pale, with a bright blue enameled stove and matching stools.

You do not have to literally commit to two colors, however. There is no prescribed color quota, and projects often evolve. In fact, this simple two-tone palette ran the risk of being too harmonious for a rule breaker like me. I could not resist upsetting the perfection, just slightly, by introducing a surprise: vibrant lime green wainscoting in the foyer off the dining room.

12.
color
balance

hen Wall Street executive John Russo and his wife, Melissa, decided to turn their weekend house into their primary residence, they were following a long-standing local tradition of urban dwellers' answering the call of country life.

The Russos loved the quirky charm of River House, which they bought a few years ago. But once they resolved to make it their full-time home, they

FRESH START: The living room's three-color palette of lime, plum, and mango makes a cheerful setting for the Russo family. Drab brown paneled walls were painted lime-tinged white to lighten the room; beams were left unpainted for a rustic contrast.

wanted to modernize the color palette to suit their own lively personalities, while at the same time respecting the history and evolution of the nineteenth-century farmhouse. The couple preserved most of the original footprint and many eccentricities, including steps of different heights, rooms that connect without halls, randomly placed windows, homemade kitchen cupboards, and vintage bathroom fittings.

COLOR CONTINUITY: The red paisley of the dining room's rug and curtains *(left)* echoes the living room's plum sofas, which can be seen in the background. Adding a touch of a single repeating color to each room gives a multicolored house a feeling of unity.

LOFTY RETREAT: A daybed in the master bedroom *(above)* is covered in vibrant fabrics, creating a colorful retreat near a two-tiered window.

ROOM MEANT FOR ROMPING: The sitting room, just off the kitchen, functions as a play area, and the family wanted it to be light, fun, and even a little silly. The former parlor, recalls designer Jennifer Johnston-Gawlik, "had awful wallpaper and dull woodwork," but rich grape-colored paint and shades of pale green and fuchsia turned the room into an entertaining, modern children's space.

Working with interior designer Jennifer Johnston-Gawlik, the Russos created a style for their country life, boldly combining their love of art and the outdoors into a vivid color scheme. The resulting visual energy matches the buzz of activity generated by a house filled with four children, aged one to seven.

"We had an overall scheme for the house," says Johnston-Gawlik, "and it consisted of blues, greens, and reds." Lest that

MOOD BOARD: Laying out the colors and materials (*above*) guided the color scheme for the landing.
HAPPY LANDING: A landing (*right*) can present a perfect— but often overlooked—opportunity to make a decorating statement. Here, a striped chair, upholstered in two different fabrics, coordinates with a river-themed accent rug.

combination sound too primary, the designer points out that it took the form of blues that were really violets, greens that were lime flavored, and reds the color of nasturtiums. Once these hues were layered over the existing architectural features—from bead board paneling to bay windows to exposed ceiling beams—the result was a house imbued with the joy of color. The country life continues to provide a refuge, and in this house, it is a colorful one.

SPLASHED WITH COLOR: The bathroom *(above)* embraces the house's cheerful color scheme. Lime green walls and multihued checked bench cushions give the master bath a zesty look.
FLORAL FUN: A guest bedroom's neutral walls and dark doorways *(right)* are enlivened by a plethora of floral patterns—in rugs, bed linens, even the lampshade.

IN THE SKY
LIKE A DIAMOND
WORL... UGH
UP A THE
WI... U ARE
HO... ONDER
LI... STAR
TWIN... E TWINKLE
U V W X Y Z ★
...N O P Q R S T

START WITH A STRIPE: The choice of a palette that includes a range of pinks in this second-floor bedroom *(left)* began with the paneling. The wide boards were painted in alternating stripes of cream and magenta, giving the wall some visual weight in a room whose steeply angled ceiling might otherwise steal the show.

HOP TO IT: For a whimsical touch on the stairway *(above)*—and to send the children up to bed with a sweet sentiment—the words to "Twinkle, Twinkle, Little Star" were painted on the stair risers. There was room left over for the alphabet on the bottom steps.

TOUCH OF BLUE:
In this second-floor bedroom, the vintage beds are tucked under the eaves, and the window trim and molding are painted blue to emphasize the architecture. Mixed patterns of varying scales decorate the linens. The overall palette is blue and red.

COLOR INGENUITY: COLOR BALANCE

BALANCING STRONG COLORS TAKES DECISION AND A DEFT HAND

Balancing colors is always part juggling act, part leap of faith. But balancing strong colors makes the leap even more perilous. Simply having a lot of colors does not mean they will perform the way you want.

Any color has a set of attributes, logical associates, and appropriate territory. Whether it is bright or soft, pastel or saturated, clear or complex, it will work best if it stays with familiar friends. Mild colors can be upset and diminished with the introduction of a loud mate. Vivid colors make gentle ones look drab or even dismayingly muddy.

Balanced colors within the same family won't overpower one another. Colors change depending on what they are next to, and a balanced palette ensures harmonious relationships.

Warm and cool colors can be mixed so long as they enrich each other. A strong palette can benefit from paler versions to lighten things up, whereas a less aggressive palette calls for saturated accents to create contrast.

A room's colors are also balanced by other elements, like wood and stone, as well as other neutrals, essential to support the weight of the color.

The main colors in the Russo living room are variations of green, plum, and yellow. While this energetic room is not for the faint of heart, it works because the colors share the same value and authority and because there are enough neutrals—walls, ceiling, floor—to anchor the vivid colors.

13.
thinking
in threes

THE PROJECT: Family treasures are reinvented with new colors for a kitchen renovation.

THE COLOR SCHEME: Teal, Dutch blue, gold, and lime green

THE INSPIRATION: Decorative tiles and pottery bought in Spain and France

WHAT WENT RIGHT: Opening up a small kitchen and separate dining room into one big room paved the way for a colorful outlook.

SENTIMENTAL FAVORITE: The Tiffany lampshade in the kitchen is a family heirloom.

JUST FOR FUN: Grandmother's antique armchair gets a golden facelift.

Anne Lemos Edgerton and her family have lived in a number of far-flung locales over the years, including Hawaii, Switzerland, and France. Anne is a composer, choreographer, and music teacher, and her husband, José, is a professor of neuro- science. With their two children in tow, Anne found herself buying colorful tiles and pottery during their sojourns in Spain and France, certain that someday her family would stay in one place long enough to put them to decorative use. That day finally arrived when,

BRIGHT IN BACK: The kitchen's teal walls, bold rugs, midnight-blue granite countertop, and cobalt tableware reinforce the palette inspired by a tile found in Spain. Providing another teal accent is the much-loved Tiffany lampshade hanging over the kitchen table; the shade once belonged to Anne's grandmother. "When it's illuminated, it has the exact color of blue as the wall," says Edgerton.

now settled in a city suburb, Anne took on the remodeling of their awkward kitchen.

Combining the kitchen and dining room into one big room created a new, light-filled space with windows on three sides. The kitchen cabinets are white with glass doors, and Anne knew from the beginning that she would build her palette around them. "I chose the main kitchen colors based on one of the tiles I found in Spain," says Edgerton, who installed the Moorish-motif tile on a backsplash wall and gave the room an overall palette of teal, blue, and yellow. This part of the house is now a vibrant gathering spot that can accommodate the books and sports gear of two school-age children as well as the aesthetic sensibilities of their parents.

Inspired by the success of her new kitchen colors, Anne gave the living its own three-color transformation with yellow, pink, and green. As comfortable as ever, the room is now alive with color.

FLOWER POWER: The bold colors of a floral area rug give a dramatic lift to the living room's main color scheme of gold, green, and pink. The hardwood floors and window casings retain their natural wood tones, while the inside of the front door is painted a dark green.

COLOR INGENUITY: THINKING IN THREES

THREE IS A HAPPY CROWD IN COLOR SCHEMES

Three colors—the concept has a nice ring. It's more interesting than two—the time-honored blue and white, for example— yet it's restrictive enough to create a clear focus for the other elements of the decoration: texture, contrast, and balance. And it allows you to pick just one more, a boon for those of us who suffer from indecision and a surfeit of options.

"Threes" can be three different colors—for example, green, yellow, and pink—or three shades of the same color. One of the colors might be a neutral, gray, or black. All three can be balanced in feel—saturated or deep tones, for example—or you might prefer a dark, a light, and an in-between shade. They may be neighbors on the standard color wheel or opposites.

You might want two warms and a cool color, or two cool colors and a warm. Any combination you come up with can work.

Thinking in threes will help you both pick colors and decide what the relative proportion of the colors should be. Ideally, the dominant color will contribute about 60 percent of the visual effect, the second color 30 percent, and the third the remaining 10 percent. The third color can have a big impact as an accent color, as a single bright wall or with some spicy pillows. Additional colors can be incorporated in tiny doses. In this small, suburban house, the eat-in kitchen and hall feature a trio of blue, teal, and yellow, while the living room is green, yellow, and pink.

THE PROJECT: A city condo showcases the collections of its well-traveled owners.

THE COLOR SCHEME: Delphinium blue, lime green, azure, leaf green, and lemon yellow

THE INSPIRATION: The homeowners' love of Asian folk art, textiles, and ceramics

WHAT WENT RIGHT: The colors of a collection of contemporary glassware displayed on white shelves play off the strong blue walls.

STARTING POINT: An abundance of neutrals— white walls, wood floors—interrupted by the fire-engine red walls of one room

JUST FOR FUN: An atrium-like upstairs area was given lemon yellow walls.

Although historic brownstones still line Boston's Back Bay, most of the Brahmin dowagers have long since given way to young families and professional couples with an eye for the modern. Kathryn Graven and Dennis Encarnation are one such couple. Having lived for many years in Asia, they and their two young sons, aged six and eight, make their home in a Boston brownstone. Finding life in their new city a bit serious, the couple worked with designer Jennifer Lobach to add some vitality to the space, a duplex

PAINTED PIZZAZZ: Walls painted lime green and delphinium blue transform the open-plan living-dining area of an urban town house. The homeowners' collections of vases and contemporary glassware make for a colorful display, while the open kitchen is reflected in the mirror above the fireplace.

with dramatic wall and ceiling planes that were created when the old floor plan was reconfigured. "They wanted a home that was charming and energizing and fun to come home to," recalls Lobach, describing her assignment. Both levels of the duplex were predominantly neutral at the start of the project, but the owners' collections reflected their eclectic taste, with ceramics and textiles acquired in Japan, Cambodia, Thailand, and Mexico. "There were already some bright colors in the rugs and accessories so we knew we could do some fun, crazy colors on the walls," says Lobach.

MOODY BLUES: Earthenware cups and bowls in muted shades of blue and green *(above)* were collected by the owners in Japan and Mexico.
GOING UP: Two shades of lavender and blue run along the stair rail *(right)* from the ground-floor entry up to the top of the duplex. The blues link the green paint in the living room with the flat brick of the staircase wall. White trim and doors and pale wood floors act as part of the color scheme.

"I love color, and I wanted our house to look like a family lives here," says Graven. The scope of the project was limited to paint, since the furnishings were already in place. The palette of blues and greens was mixed and repeated, sometimes on a single angled wall, sometimes across a whole room.

As is typical in brownstones, the walls along one side of the duplex are brick. Two shades of lavender and blue were used along the solid stair railing. "We've found that peri-winkles and purples complement the brick found in many Boston town houses," says Lobach.

High ceilings are another brown-stone feature, and the use of color on the walls, particularly in bands of blue above the built-in display shelves, breaks up the height. The walls of the first-floor living room alternate in zones between a pale green and a delphinium blue. At one end of the dining area, a single hot orange wall provides a vivid back-drop for a set of multicolored rustic chairs and a painted hutch. The din-ing room's bay window has an upholstered seat and doubles as a place for the boys to play.

DINING IN THE GLOW: The rustic-style multicolored hutch in the dining room was the inspiration for the vivid orange wall. Rush-seated chairs in bright colors and a stone-topped dining table are lively and informal.

On the second floor, a central skylight illuminates the space. Tall interior glass walls let light into the small rooms and play up the colors within.

Throughout the home, the couple's many collections add personality and texture. The shine of glass vases, the luster of pottery glazes, and the warmth of embroidered hangings from Asia and Mexico soften the strongly colored walls and bring a human scale to the soaring ceilings. Says Graven, "We live in New England, so having a brightly colored house makes all the difference."

BRIGHT BOX: A large skylight illuminates the rooms and open staircase on the upper level *(above)*. Glass interior walls allow the room colors to shine out, and the blue paint from the stairway below mirrors the summer sky above.

FAR EAST LULLABY: The spicy guest bedroom *(right)* features a futon bed and vibrant textiles, all from Japan.

SPRING DREAMS: Striking leaf green walls and pillows *(above)* combine with the bed-covering's pink design to compose a springtime theme in the master bedroom.

WATER ZONE: Painting just one wall can be an effective way to delineate space *(right)*. Here, a single yellow wall abuts a single teal one, with the bathroom appearing through a graphic white doorway. The blue and green floor tiles supply extra color saturation, while the white architectural trim and fixtures emphasize the geometry.

COLOR INGENUITY: **COLOR ZONES**

COLOR BLOCKS
CREATE DEFINITION
IN AIRY, OPEN
FLOOR PLANS

Many families today prefer the casual feel of an open floor plan. The challenge from a decorative standpoint is how to define a large area so it isn't one endless monochromatic space that offers no rest for the eye.

In this remodeled condo, various walls were taken down and a staircase added to create a duplex. An untraditional layout resulted, and the owners, with their extensive and colorful art collections, were not content to settle for the easy-out of all white. Blocking out color zones on walls proved an effective way to define spaces and create a purpose and identity for each.

Few rooms here have the classic four walls and a door, but the inventive design approach highlighted single walls and

angled planes to create a three-dimensional play of color on multiple levels. Variations on a blue/pale green theme crisscross the lower level and continue up the stairs. The long wall that runs from living room to dining room to street-facing bay window was broken out into zones of blue, red, and yellow—color acting as a virtual room divider.

Color zones can be used almost anywhere. Even traditionally shaped rooms can be invigorated by a single wall with a flash of color. Ceilings, floors, doors, and staircases can all become zones for color playfulness. Architecture is enhanced and emphasized when organized in color zones.

15.
color
placement

ed and all its warm connotations figure prominently in the palette of a Vermont house whose owners wanted a warm, casual feeling for their weekend retreat. The house, surrounded by stone walls and gardens, sits on a sunny hilltop near a ski resort and is a favorite escape for this transplanted English couple and their grown children and guests. A renovation added square footage to the original structure, replacing a tiny galley kitchen with

STRIPES AND CHECKS: Three versions of zesty red fabric were used to upholster the chairs, featuring stripes at the big dining table and checks in the adjacent, sunny breakfast room. For large parties, both tables are used.

a larger one that opens onto a lofty great room designed for dining and casual gathering. A new breakfast area with walls of windows and French doors was built off the great room, giving the family an intimate garden-view table that can also accommodate the overflow at larger dinner parties. The great room features cathedral ceilings and exposed beams, while the kitchen and breakfast-area addition have a homier scale, with eight-foot ceilings.

The palette of coral red, teal, and yellow ties the various spaces together. The walls in the great room were painted a soft teal, and the same color was used for the transitional

PALETTE PERSPECTIVE: A view of the dining table, looking toward the entry hall *(above)*, shows three of the major hues in the house's color scheme: geranium red chairs, yellow draperies, and teal walls. The blue-painted hutch that can be glimpsed in the entry hall is a late-1800s Russian antique with original paint.

COLOR DETAIL: Echoing the room's glow, a tangerine nestles in a vintage pink pressed-glass cup atop a glass serving plate *(right).*

doorways into the breakfast area and kitchen. Set off by the room's warm reds and yellows, the teal almost becomes a neutral. The yellow of the great room draperies is repeated in a lighter shade in the breakfast area. A trio of red fabrics—one plaid, one striped, one solid—was chosen for the dining and breakfast-area chairs, which can thus be moved around interchangeably. And for a quirky color splash, the base of the kitchen island that faces the great room was color-matched to the red fabric of the chairs.

During the renovation, the house's four small upstairs bedrooms were transformed into two bedroom suites. In the master suite, an exposed post provided a motif for a decorative artist who painted faux wood posts and beams along one entire wall. When other family members or friends come to stay,

COZY IN TERRA-COTTA: The overall palette continues across the hall in the living room's glazed terra-cotta walls, antique side table, and teal upholstery. The random-width pine floors and stone fireplace were existing elements in the house. Decorative painter Nancy McKeegan created the stencil design for the shutters, an attractive alternative to fabric window treatments.

they can choose among three additional bedrooms in a guesthouse on the ten-acre property.

The warm color palette of coral and teal is picked up again on the other side of the house, where there is an intimate living room with a massive stone fireplace and a piano. Opting for interior shutters instead of more traditional window treatments, the home owners had a local artist reinterpret motifs from the room's rug as a decorative painted stencil, a folk effect perfect for this country getaway.

BY THE WINDOW: Two small rush stools *(above)* sit under the stenciled shutters.

SOOTHING STEPS: The main entry *(right)* features a neutral color scheme that plays up the architectural details and serves as a staging area for the colorful rooms that open off it.

Throughout the house, antique furniture with original painted finishes adds another color presence. Like everything else here, the well-worn patina of these pieces, which include a hutch in the entry hall and a table in the living room, contribute to an overwhelming sense of comfort.

TRUE OR FAUX?: Only one of the posts and beams in the master bedroom *(left)* is real; the others were painted in trompe l'oeil style to add visual interest and a bit of humor to the tan walls. The genuine post is to the left of the bed.

GUEST RETREAT: A bedroom in the guesthouse *(above)* is decorated with lively fabrics and colors, including a striped Roman shade, a bright yellow dresser, and a sea-creature-themed rug and pillows. The light yellow wall color relates to the painted dresser.

COLOR INGENUITY: COLOR PLACEMENT

COLORS CREATE ENERGY IN POSITIVE AND NEGATIVE SPACE; MANAGE IT CAREFULLY

Color placement considers all the factors that will make a project successful. Included are the relative importance of each color, the way contrasting colors define a room's shape and fittings, the way colors transition from room to room, and how the setting (light, architecture, materials) directs you.

I create a project board that includes visual references for all the elements involved. Take a digital photo of the room and mark it up with big arrows and a shopping list, showing everything from ceiling to floor, woodwork to doors. Photograph, sketch, or cut from a magazine placeholders for the main furnishings: for example, upholstery for living rooms, beds and dressers for bedrooms, and so on. The more specific the framework you create for your color chips, the easier it will be to visualize the room.

Now comes the fun part: shuffling the colors the way you would compose a picture. One comfortable option is to mimic nature. Use a light color for the ceiling (the sky), a medium value for the walls (the forest), and a darker color for the floor (the ground). Furniture should fill the space but not crowd it. Window treatments should do their job but not distract from the room's architecture.

This open living space, combining kitchen, dining room, and breakfast room, placed color in decisive blocks of teal (walls), red (chairs), and yellow (draperies), with a white ceiling and a dark floor.

RESOURCES

Susan Sargent
3609 Main Street
Manchester Village, VT 05254
800-245-4767 or 802-366-4955
www.susansargent.com

rugs, bedding, pillows, furniture, lamps, dinnerware, fabrics, trims, wallpaper, paints, decorative accessories, and interior design services

Fine Paints of Europe
P.O. Box 419
Woodstock, VT 05091
800-332-1556
www.finepaintsofeurope.com

Susan Sargent paints

Robert Allen–Beacon Hill
Decoration & Design Building
979 Third Avenue, 3rd floor
New York, NY 10022
212-421-1200
www.robertallendesign.com

Susan Sargent fabrics

FABRIC
Susan Sargent
3609 Main Street
Manchester Village, VT 05254
800-245-4767 or 802-366-4955
www.susansargent.com

Country Swedish
Decoration & Design Building
979 Third Avenue, Suite 1409
New York, NY 10022
212-838-1976
www.countryswedish.com

chapter 6

HAND-BLOCKED WALLPAPER
Adelphi Paper Hangings
P.O. Box 494
The Plains, VA 20198
540-253-5367
www.adelphipaperhangings.com

order Adelphi papers through
Steve Larson
102 Main Street
P.O. Box 135
Sharon Springs, NY 13459
518-284-9066

chapter 11

PAINTED FURNITURE
Maine Cottage
www.mainecottage.com

chapter 12

DECORATIVE CERAMIC ACCESSORIES
Cyclamen Collection
510-434-7620
www.cyclamencollection.com

chapter 15

TILES
Roseberry-Winn Pottery and Tile
3842 Main Road
Tiverton, RI 02878
401-816-0010
www.roseberrywinn.com

chapter 11

KITCHEN CABINETS
Bill Holmolka
Vermont Custom Kitchens
802-362-1723
customkitchen1@verizon.net

chapter 11

RECYCLED FLOORING
Longleaf Lumber
115 Fawcett Street
Cambridge, MA 02138
617-871-6611
www.longleaflumber.com

chapter 11

INTERIOR DESIGNERS

Jennifer Johnston-Gawlik
Perennial Studio
Pawlet, VT
802-724-9001
flowers@vermontel.net

chapters 1, 12

Marian Glasgow
Marian Glasgow Interiors
9 Laurel Street
Newton Center, MA 02459
617-965-0936

chapter 2

Mary Jo Gourd
3546 Main Street
P.O. Box 300
Manchester Village, VT 05254
802-362-1480
www.ramsaygourdarchitects.com

chapters 8, 15

Jennifer J. Lobach and Colleen J. Rosar
Mandara Associates, Inc.
246 Marlborough Street #3
Boston, MA 02116
617-848-3977
mandarainteriors@gmail.com

chapter 14

Gayle Wells Mandle
Providence, RI
gmandle@risd.edu

chapter 3

Leah Robins Designs
10 Bailey Road
Watertown, MA 02472
617-926-8660
lrobins@rcn.com

chapter 5

ARCHITECTS

Ramsay Gourd Architects
3546 Main Street
P.O. Box 300
Manchester Village, VT 05254
802-362-1480
www.ramsaygourdarchitects.com

chapters 8, 15

N. Thomas Warner
63 Court Street
Middlebury, VT 05753
802-388-2550

chapter 1

PAINTERS

Matt Cote
Lukin Murals
info@ilovelukin.com

murals in the New England area;
chapter 6

Stan Wambolt
Colors Painting
508-981-5456 or 508-357-9813

Boston area; chapter 6

Nancy McKeegan
979 Frost Hill Road
Belmont, VT 05730
802-259-3333

decorative stencils; chapter 15

INSPIRATIONS

Barefoot Books
2067 Massachusetts Avenue
Cambridge, MA 02140
617-576-0660
www.barefootbooks.com

chapter 9

INDEX

ACKNOWLEDGMENTS

With thanks for the wonderful support of Sarah Parke; Gary Gras;
John Lahey; handy Stan Wamboldt; my always supportive husband, Tom Peters;
and pal and color cohort, Eric Roth.